My ATTACK Planner

Feel free to share this – just don't try to pass it off as your own! If you enjoy this guidebook and find it helpful, I really hope you'll do me the favor of leaving a review. You can connect with us at www.ATTACKBball.com or www.facebook.com/ATTACKBball.

Foreword

"I am pleased to both support and recommend My ATTACK Planner to you. As an 11-time world champion boxer and Olympic medalist, I believe in utilizing sports to instill determination and resilience. We must allow athletes to impact themselves and others far beyond the game. Therefore, I consistently emphasize mental toughness and the importance of preparation. For every hour an athlete physically prepares, I recommend at least four hours of mental preparation. My concentration on process over outcomes is how I was able to achieve championships in 4 different weight classes.

As a parent of a basketball player, I am excited to instill the nuggets of wisdom this book provides into my son. Coach Charlie Miller has prepared a well-thought out guidebook that not only details a physical process that I will implement for my own son, but also aids in developing a growth mindset. The mindset is the key to becoming passionate about the process and unlocking the best version of the athlete both on and off the court.

All sports, including the game of basketball, are forever evolving. Players today must possess physical and mental skillsets for all five basketball positions to be considered exceptional. In this book, Coach Charlie does an excellent job of explaining the fundamentals of basketball while incorporating current holistic training and conditioning techniques. Coach Charlie uses this book to paint a clear picture of how to develop a complete player. Players can apply this information to their year-

round training regimen and, after developing mental strength, stay true to their style of play under any coaching system.

In conclusion, this book is a compilation of the lessons learned, the trials and errors, and successes of Coach Charlie's 30+ year basketball journey. I can vouch for his basketball prowess, mental fortitude, and leadership skills. Now all you must do is follow this MAP to the other side of success."

Roy Jones Jr.,
11-Time World Boxing Champion

"*My relationship with Charlie goes back to our childhood growing up in Miami. Basketball is what grew our relationship and to this day has taken it to another level. I can still remember our days of playing against each other in high school and all the way through college, with Charlie at the University of Indiana and myself at the University of Kentucky. Charlie is not only a great friend but has a great basketball mind. I never walk away from a conversation with Charlie and not learn something about the game of basketball and the game of life. I remember when Charlie shared the idea with me about this book, and as usual how excited he was to share what he has learned with the world. This book is a gift to the basketball world. No matter where you're at in your basketball journey this book is a must read, and a book that you should refer back to frequently. My ATTACK Planner is a book that should be passed down from generation to generation. Charlie has taken player development to the next level with this book. He teaches you techniques and fundamentals with basketball terminology that's easy to understand. You will understand how and why you're doing what you're doing.*"

Allen Edwards
Men's Basketball Head Coach
University of Wyoming

Preface

"Believe it or not, I used to be a skinny, uncoordinated kid that got picked last for most sports. I never dreamed of playing basketball in middle school, much less at the collegiate or professional levels. The difference is that I made a choice to become the best basketball player I could be and to put in the work to achieve my goal.

This book is so special to me because it is the result of all the hours I spent training in the gym, and preparing for and playing in games all over the world as a player. All of my experiences as a player over the last 25 years allowed me to research, quantify, and produce implementable systems as a coach.

Now, instead of you having to go through the trials and tribulations of determining how best to train on your own, I am providing you with a blueprint on a silver platter. I know I cannot personally train everyone, so this book gives me a way to reach many more players who have a goal of playing basketball at the next level.

I feel honored to have had all the experiences that allow me to write this book, and I believe the reason for my journey is to pass on my knowledge and to help mentor others. This is why you need to use and appreciate this guide!!!"

Coach Charlie Miller
President, ATTACK Basketball Academy

Table of Contents

Work Your Plan and Plan Your Work

"The key is not the will to win... everybody has that. It is the will to prepare to win that is important."

The purpose of a planner is to keep you organized and on top of your priorities. I developed this planner for you to use on your basketball journey. You should use this on a daily basis, so as soon as you wake up you know exactly what you have to do for the day. It will also keep your day balanced as you can schedule time for your basketball workout, school, and fun with your friends. So, let's talk about why EVERYONE needs a planner.

What happens when you DON'T have a planner?

1. Your to-dos are to-don'ts — because you will forget your tasks and never complete them.
2. You are the master of excuses — it's easy to explain why something wasn't finished when it wasn't written down.
3. You have wishes but no set goals — very few people achieve goals that aren't written.
4. You don't put in the work — you want to be the superstar without the sweat equity.
5. You are stressed — you are so disorganized that even the thought of a planner causes you anxiety.

6. You have blinders on – you are trying to keep your head above water to manage the next task that someone throws at you. You never have time to look at your bigger picture or long-term goals.

Why is developing and sticking to a plan important?

1. You are accountable – a plan shows you whether you are still on the correct road to arrive at your final destination.
2. Your to-dos are all in one place – you aren't hunting for Post-it notes around the house to remind yourself of your last great idea.
3. You create protected time – you set aside specific amounts of time to complete tasks so they don't seem as daunting.
4. You can still be flexible – you can change and update your plans when life happens.
5. You categorize what's important – you will make time for the important things. If it's not worth your time, don't include it in your planner!
6. You follow the breadcrumbs to your goal – you can celebrate each milestone achieved on the way to your goal.

Praise Your Effort

Planning is important, but praising yourself along the way is just as integral to your success. What do I mean? I mean praising yourself for reaching each step along the way. You should be just as ecstatic about the effort you put into achieving your goal as reaching the actual goal itself. Doing this allows you to put more emphasis on your effort than the result. This way, if you do achieve your goal, you praise yourself for your effort AND your achievement. But, if you fall short of your goal, you are still able to praise yourself for your effort. Recognizing your effort allows you to be proud of yourself for stepping outside your comfort zone and doing something you don't normally do. Then you can ask a parent, mentor, teacher, etc., for guidance on how you can modify your plan to hit a new goal.

Taking the time to stop and praise your efforts, instead of waiting for others to praise you, makes it much more likely for you to reach for lofty goals. Instead of being preoccupied with pleasing others, you will be driven to go for what you believe in.

Why Goal Setting?

A goal is an aim or a desired result. Having goals inspires you to take action. So, on days when you have no motivation to work, your goals will you along. However, having goals in your head isn't enough, as unwritten goals are just wishes. This book is here to help you turn your wishes into attainable goals. To properly set a goal, you want to be SMART about it.

S – Specific. You need to be specific with your goal by defining the "what," "how," and "why" (e.g., by March 24 I will make 3,000 shots by making 100 shots per day for 30 days, so I can increase my shooting percentage and take more risks during games).

Example Breakdown:

The what: "By March 24 I will make 3,000 shots"

The how: "by making 100 per day for 30 days"

The why: "so I can increase my shooting percentage and take more risks during games"

This is important because it helps you create a daily sense of urgency on the path toward achieving your goal.

M – Measurable. Your goal needs to be measurable so you have tangible evidence of your journey. Using the same example above, your daily milestones are your 100 made shots, and your ultimate measurable is whether you meet your 3,000 made shots by March 24.

A – Attainable. Your goal should be attainable, but should stretch you into an uncomfortable zone. Coach Billy Donovan from the Oklahoma City Thunder once said he doesn't think it's possible for people to grow without adversity. The discomfort of adversity gives you a push, and your view of it as an opportunity propels you to your goal. Using the example above, making 3,000 shots is an attainable goal because making 100 shots per day is realistic. Shooting 10 sets of shots with 10 makes per set equals 100 per day.

R – Results focused. You want to focus on the bigger picture, and not get caught up in the minutia of the activities. This way when you face adversity on your journey, you can see past it and continue towards your final destination. This reminds you that there is a light at the end of the tunnel. The big-picture result in the example we have been using is: "I will make 3,000 shots."

T – Timely. Your goal should have a deadline to hold you accountable and to create a practical sense of urgency. The deadline in the example we have been using is: "March 24."

As I mentioned in the "Results focused" description, you WILL face adversity on your journey. When this happens, you should rely on the guidance of Triple A:

1. Acknowledge the adversity – Take a moment to recognize what happened. Adversity is NOT a bad thing, so don't label it that way. But don't pretend it didn't happen, either. Simply take note of what occurred.

2. Assess the situation – All is NOT lost when adversity happens, so don't throw your planner in the trash. If you are on a road trip and you run into traffic, you don't turn around and go home! The same concept applies here. Carefully look at your original plan, taking into account your bump in the road, and look at alternative routes. Alternative routes are called best practices, which are go-to solutions for inevitable challenging situations.

3. Adjust your game plan – After determining the best new road to take to your goal, adjust your written plan and be on your way!

Using the SMART method of goal setting gives you something tangible to follow on a daily basis. By simply using this planner, you are in the top three percent of the population. According to a Harvard MBA study, only three percent of people have written, specific goals! 83 percent of people have NO goals at all. Stop making excuses and be the exception to the rule! And if you think you don't have time to write down your goals, just think about the time you will spend sitting the bench...

Personal Goals

My goal is to:

_____

_____

_____

(e.g., by March 24 I will make 3,000 shots by making 100 shots per day for 30 days, so I can increase my shooting percentage and take more risks during games. Remember the SMART goal-setting rules and be specific!)

I will accomplish this by:

_____

_____

_____

_____

_____

_____

_____

(Write a detailed action plan to accomplish your goals. Include target dates for when you want to hit certain milestones.)

Accountability partners are people who you can rely on to keep you on track to hit your goals. They will provide emotional support but will NOT feel sorry for you when you rattle off a list of excuses about why you didn't do your task for the day. Accountability partners are people who will keep you moving forward when you feel overwhelmed or stuck. They will help you get out of your own way, kick your butt from time to time, but will also be your cheerleader. Now that you understand what to look for in an accountability partner, think of two people you know who you can rely on. Once you have asked and they have accepted their duties, write their names down!

These people will be my accountability partners:

Name: _____

Name: _____

The Self-Interview

Now that we have discussed goal setting, we need to develop our mindset. In order to ready your mind for your journey, you must determine what you are willing to commit to in order to achieve your goal. Committing to your goal means there are some things you will have to give up in order to devote adequate time to achieving your goal. Committing to your goal is important because it states that you are dedicated to your plan and to your final goal, no matter what happens.

You should commit to your goal in writing, so when you get tired on the way to your goal, you can refer back to your written commitment and gain the energy needed to continue on your path.

This is where the "self-interview" comes into play. You should go to a quiet place, this could be somewhere as simple as your bedroom, ask yourself questions, and answer them *honestly*. The following are suggestions for questions you can ask yourself during your interview to get you on the right track. Feel free to add any questions that pertain to your specific situation.

Why am I trying to reach these goals?

Are my goals going to stretch me?

What are my priorities?

Am I willing to dedicate the time needed to achieve my goals?

Am I willing to reallocate time from other activities or social engagements to achieve my goals?

Do I have a support group to help me on my path to achieve my goals?

What will be likely to hinder me in achieving my goals?

This self-interview will make you aware that the journey you are about to embark on is your decision and no one else's. Now that you understand the importance of a well-thought-out plan, you have written your goals, and you have developed your mindset, you are ready to begin your physical journey!

Mental Toughness

Do you find yourself playing with a lot of nervous energy? Sitting on the bench after putting your all into training? Being afraid to step up when the team needs you? Being so anxious that you can't think straight? This stops TODAY! This planner is designed to help you become your authentic self and to finally play the way you have always envisioned.

All of these blockages arise from a lack of mental conditioning. Many basketball players focus so much on the primary aspect of the sport (the physical skills), that the assumption is that the secondary aspect (mental toughness) will automatically develop. This is not your fault, as this is what most coaches are taught to focus on. Unfortunately, it is a myth! You have to actively develop your mind in order to become an elite player.

Players who do not condition their minds are the ones who won't take risks, overthink their actions, and second-guess themselves. These are the players that are on the bench more than they are on the court. Simply put, coaches can get over physical mistakes, but not mental ones. Your physical skills can be a level 10, but if your mental skills are a level 2, no one will ever see the work you put into your physical skills. This is because it is IMPOSSIBLE for you to perform your skills with your mind holding you back. You have heard the saying, "A chain is only as strong as its weakest link." Don't let your mind be your weak link.

The great news is that, just like any other muscle in your body, you can also do exercises to strengthen your mind. A lot of what I have touched on already (goal setting, self-interview, written planning) will help you do just this. Other examples of tasks you can do to condition your mind are to play memory games, spend 15 minutes per day meditating, and practice daily affirmations. These will help your mind remain focused on your current task, instead of wandering off and thinking about something that has nothing to do with what you are doing at the present time. If you are on the court, your mind should be too. If you are on the bench, your mind should be focused on how to best help your team from where you are currently.

Training your mind to concentrate only on the task at hand is invaluable when it comes to basketball. It strips away the "squirrel effect" of your mind getting distracted by anything and everything, and allows you to be at peace with what you are currently doing, knowing that you are doing it to the best of your ability. This sounds amazing, doesn't it? If you follow this MAP, this can be your way of life!

Memory Games

Examples of memory games you can play are as follows:

1. Use mnemonic devices – These are memory tools that give meaning and organization to a random group of concepts. I use this constantly. I use acronyms, word associations, and rhyming. For example, I use: Hips, Hands, Feet Follow to teach my players the order of how to shoot an effective, repeatable shot. Speaking this aloud while performing the actions allows players to get in sync with the shooting order more efficiently.

2. Play brain games – Break out your Sudoku book or download Roberto. It's a free app that allows you to do various brain exercises for six minutes per day. Each of these exercises is scientifically designed to improve your memory, reaction time, and ability to focus. And they are fun! Improving your reaction time allows you to respond versus reacting in games. This allows you to always be in control during a game instead of reacting to your opponent.

3. Quit multitasking - Studies show that it takes eight seconds to fully commit a piece of information to memory, so it is critical to concentrate on only the task at hand. When someone calls you on the phone, sit down and listen to what they have to say. When you are

working on the computer, only open the windows necessary for you to complete your current task. And turn off your phone so you are not distracted by notifications!

4. Master a new skill – A recent study showed that practicing any activity on a regular basis improved memory and overall brain function. This could be playing an instrument, skiing, knitting, or whatever activity you can get lost in.

5. Get more sleep – Everyone should get eight or more hours of sleep per night. It is said that this is the time the brain needs to shift memories from temporary to long-term storage. Losing just three or four hours of sleep one night can lead to fading memory. So, do yourself a favor and create a bedtime routine that will allow you to hit the sack earlier.

Meditation

Although meditation doesn't pack the same punch as a well-balanced diet or daily exercise, there is a reason why it has been around for thousands of years. Here are a few reasons why you might want to incorporate mindfulness meditation into your daily life:

1. It lowers stress – literally. The hormone your body produces in response to stress is decreased after meditation.
2. It makes your grades better – Studies show that students who practice meditation regularly do better on tests.
3. It allows you to have better control – Meditation controls the alpha waves in your brain, allowing you to have better control over processing pain and emotions. So, the next time your coach gives you feedback on areas for improvement, you can process the information without having an emotional breakdown.
4. It makes you a better person – Practicing meditation can benefit the people you interact with by making you more compassionate. More meditation equals more do-good behavior.
5. It helps you when you are not actively practicing – You do not have to be in the act of meditating for it to still benefit your brain's emotional processing. So, just like your body reaps the benefits of exercising long after your

workout is over, your mind reaps the benefits of meditation long after you roll up your mat.

Recently an elementary school in Baltimore implemented meditation instead of detention. Students that got into trouble were sent to the Mindful Moment Room, where they were instructed to breathe deeply, close their eyes, sit quietly, and then discuss why they were there. This room has done wonders for the school learning environment and productivity. It brings peace to the children and allows them to return to class and concentrate on their work.

This also applies to sports. Many people are not aware, but great players such as Kobe Bryant, LeBron James, and Michael Jordan practice mindful meditation. In fact, Michigan's head coach John Beilein incorporates meditation into his team's training regimen.

Following is a quick how-to guide as an introduction to meditation from www.gaiam.com:
(https://www.gaiam.com/blogs/discover/meditation-101-techniques-benefits-and-a-beginner-s-how-to)

1. Sit or lie comfortably.
2. Close your eyes.
3. Make no effort to control your breath; simply breathe naturally.
4. Focus your attention on your breath and on how your body moves with each inhalation and exhalation. Notice the movement of your body as you breathe. Observe

your chest, shoulders, rib cage, and belly. Simply focus your attention on your breath without controlling its pace or intensity. If your mind wanders, return your focus back to your breath.

Maintain this meditation practice for two to three minutes to start, and then try it for longer periods.

You can also search for "guided meditation" on YouTube and listen to these audio recordings while meditating. These are often easier for beginners as there is a voice talking throughout the meditation, which guides you and helps to keep your mind on track. There are guided meditations for almost any subject (releasing anxiety, increasing your sports performance, going to sleep, etc.) If you search for it, you can find it.

So, the next time you are upset, stressed, or mad about something, I suggest meditating to get your mind in a state where you are confident and ready to face the world!

Affirmations

What exactly are affirmations? Simply put, they are powerful sentences aimed to influence your mind. They are designed to energize and inspire you to action. The key to affirmations is in the repetition. You have to say them so often that you not only believe in them, but you have become them. This is called auto-suggestion, which means your subconscious mind is now influencing your habits, actions, and responses. Affirmations can help you train harder, develop a positive mindset, and progress more quickly to your goals.

It is ideal to have a special, quiet time to repeat your affirmations to yourself. However, the great thing about them is that you can repeat them anywhere and anytime. The more, the better.

When creating your affirmations, ask yourself if you really want to achieve them. If you have doubts, you will NOT get what you want. These doubts will act as mental roadblocks that you physically will not be able to get around. Don't get discouraged if your mind generates doubts; this is natural. The important part is that you persevere and do not allow your negative thoughts to take over. Defer to your affirmations for guidance.

Affirmations should always be written in the present tense. This means they should start with "I am," "I always," "I do," etc. This is important because you want to put yourself in your target scenario right NOW. If you say, "I will be...", it is impossible for you to imagine yourself at your end-goal because you are affirming the feeling of wanting instead of the feeling of already having what you desire.

Affirmations should also be written based on what you want, not on avoiding what you do not want. For example, instead of saying, "I don't want to fail my class", say, "I am an excellent student and earning high grades comes easy to me." It's all about conditioning your mind to think about what is possible for you.

Some sample affirmations for sports are as follows:

I make sure to always push myself

I am the difference-maker on my team

I am willing to do what it takes to improve

I always work hard

I am an amazing athlete

Quadrants of Training

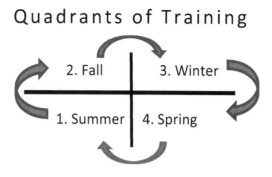

2. Fall	3. Winter
1. Summer	4. Spring

If you want to separate yourself from other players and become exceptional from a holistic standpoint (mind, body, and soul), you have to train based on the seasons. You should be training on 90-day cycles. Why 90 days? Because the first 30-day phase is creating a habit, meaning your body and mind are accepting your workout routine. The second 30-day phase is building the habit, meaning you have to hold yourself accountable to your routine and push yourself. The third 30-day phase is becoming the habit, where your routine is a part of who you are. This means that the moves are so intuitive for you that you can easily think in action in any situation.

Your training during basketball season should not be the same as your training regimen during the off-season. Summer, Fall, and Spring seasons should all incorporate 3v3 play as part of the training regimen. 3v3 allows you to work on your skills in a game setting, an important part of training. During 3v3 games, you will get more purposeful touches on offense and will be forced to get involved defensively. These games will easily expose your weaknesses but will also build confidence as your skillset blossoms.

Suggested training for each season is detailed as follows:

Summer

The Summer is the time to work on the things you MUST improve on. I call this the Deficiency Season. This is one of the toughest seasons because you have to take the feedback and analysis from your in-season play and work on it. These are the skills that are holding you back from moving to the next level. This could mean moving from the B to the A team, making a top-tier AAU team, earning more playing time, etc.

The reason that the Summer is the time to work on your deficiencies is because you have time to recover from the mental and physical frustration and exhaustion from these workouts. For example, if the weakest part of your game is dribbling with your left hand and that is all you work on over the Summer, you will have more confidence than you can imagine when you go into the next season and surprise all of your coaches and teammates with your newfound skill. Remember, if you want to move to the next level, you CANNOT skip this season!

Fall

The Fall is the Grooving Season, which includes a lot of repetition. This is the time to solidify what you worked on over the Summer. You don't want to introduce new skills during this time because you want your mind to be relaxed going into tryouts and basketball season. I do a lot of timed drills during this season, as it is all about getting as many shots, dribbles, passes, etc., as possible during the workout.

This Grooving Season is also the perfect time to know your individual strengths and how they fit into your role on the team. Once you have created the mental and physical fortitude to perform your skills in any situation, your coach will have no choice but to play you.

<u>Winter</u>

Winter is Maintenance Season. Personally, I hate it! Here is why: 90 percent of players who train year-round are still afraid to implement what they have been learning into a game setting. If you are too afraid to take a risk in a game, there is no point in training the other three seasons. You HAVE to become emotionally connected and feel the training you do in all seasons, so you have faith and belief in yourself. You need to know that the achievement of your skillset is your goal, not how many points you score or your win-loss record.

<u>Spring</u>

Spring is Collection Season because you have to take time to recover both mentally and physically from the basketball season. This is also the time to collect your thoughts and reflect on what you did well and what you need to improve on. Talk to your coaches and teammates to get honest feedback so you know what to work on over the Summer, or Deficiency Season.

Then take the time to put together a comprehensive game plan regarding how you are going to tackle these opportunities. Prepare yourself mentally and physically for the upcoming season.

Basketball-Specific Strength/Performance Training

Just like basketball training, basketball strength training is different for each season. The duration and reps will change based on the season, but the workouts will remain the same. Basketball players should take off at least two days between strength training. The sweet spot for strength training is two to three times per week.

When you are strength training for basketball, always keep in mind what muscles you will be using during a game. Basketball players need strong legs, glutes, shoulders, core, and triceps, which will help with consistent shooting and passing during a game. The less fatigued your muscles are during a game, the more focused you will be, and you will make fewer mistakes.

Some great exercises for basketball-specific strength training are: lat pulls, triceps pulls, pushups, lunges, squats, leg curls, leg presses, chest inclines, crunches, planks, superman, cleans, and jerks. Please note that form is everything when it comes to these exercises. These exercises should be performed under the watchful eye of a coach unless you have been taught the proper form. Do not throw your back out or pull a muscle because you are tired and get out of the correct stance. Listen to your body!

During performance training, you are working on coordination, agility, and reaction. Excelling at all these

31

components is what makes a great basketball player, as you will quicken your reaction time and outlast your opponents.

Performance training should occur about three times per week and should NOT be on the same days as strength training. The reason is that you need the energy for optimal performance, which you will not have if you are tapped out from weight lifting. You should do your performance training before your basketball workout as it is a great way to get warmed up for playing. My suggestion is to have six to eight go-to performance training exercises that you can use on a regular basis.

Some examples of great performance training exercises are as follows:

<u>Drop Step Runs/Defensive Slides</u> – See diagram below

<u>4 Corners</u> – Run, Slide, Backpedal, and Sprint in a square

<u>Shuttle runs/Line Touches</u> – Run from baseline to free throw line, back to baseline, then all the way through to mid-court line

<u>17s</u> – Run sideline to sideline (up and back counts as two). The goal is to do 17 in three minutes. Do five sets of these during your workout.

<u>55</u> – Run from baseline to half court or full court (your preference) and back to the baseline (baseline to half court counts as one). The goal is to build up to 55 (1 + 2 + 3 + 4 + 5 + 6 + 7 + 8 + 9 +10) and finish in five minutes.

<u>5 Minute Jumps</u> – Jumping in place, or what I like to call low-impact bounding is your active recovery. This is what you default to between each of the following jumps: the formation of a W, the formation of a square, back-and-forth, and 360s. You should do each of these jump moves for about 10 seconds each with the whole exercise lasting for five minutes. Do not stop jumping for the five minutes!

As explained earlier, the quadrants of training also apply to strength and performance training. Here are the details of each season and how you should attack them to achieve the best results.

<u>Summer</u>
This is when you concentrate on strength training to bulk up and get stronger. You want to use more weight and do less reps. During this season, performance training will comprise the first 15 minutes of your basketball workout.

<u>Fall</u>
Your strength and performance training is now focused on endurance. This means less weight and higher reps, along with

condition runs. These are 100-, 50-, and 20-yard runs designed to increase your lung capacity. These are typically done outside on a field.

Winter

All of your workouts should be focused on injury prevention and flexibility. Your strength training exercises should be focused on core work, band work, and low weight. You should do very little performance training during this season as you are doing enough drills during practices and games. Your sole focus should be giving your all during practices and games.

Spring

This season is about rest, recover, and resistance. It is a blend of Winter and Summer when it comes to strength and performance training, as you need to give your body a rest period (I recommend about two weeks) and also gear up for your intense Summer workouts.

During the Spring, you will review what worked for you and what did not so you know what to focus your energy on for your Summer training. After your rest period, you should begin your Summer schedule around performance and strength training. Have fun with it. Find fun, innovative ways to change your training up and keep it interesting.

Aerobic vs Anaerobic

There are two different ways to train: aerobically and anaerobically. As an athlete, including both types in your training program can increase your strength, power, and endurance.

Aerobic exercise means that your muscles are getting their energy delivered to them by oxygen. This is the type of training you do to build endurance, so it involves continuous movement. In basketball, you will concentrate heavily on this type of training in the Fall season. Examples of aerobic exercises are running, swimming, or cross-country skiing. The aerobic portion of your training session should last about 15 to 20 minutes.

In order to see improvements on the basketball court, your aerobic training should mimic the movements you will make during a game. Some examples of aerobic exercises geared toward basketball are jogging while dribbling a basketball and jumping rope. As beneficial as aerobic training is for your basketball game, incorporating anaerobic training into your routine will give you what you need to excel on the court. According to the American Sports Medicine Institute, athletes who focus solely on aerobic training find that they experience a decrease in power and strength when playing their sport of choice.

So, what is anaerobic exercise? Anaerobic literally means an absence of oxygen. So, in these exercises, your muscles are getting their energy from phosphagen and lactic acids. These types of exercises are more intense, usually lasting only 30 seconds to two minutes. Examples of anaerobic exercise are heavy weight training, sprinting, and jumping. A popular anaerobic method of exercising is interval training. Interval training alternates between short bursts of high intensity activities like sprinting with lower intensity activities like squats. It is great for basketball training as it prepares you for the short bursts of speed and power you need during a game. In my opinion, interval training interspersed with aerobic training is the best recipe for basketball training.

Let's Get Physical

Now that we have worked hard on training our mind, we are ready to get our bodies involved. Before you jump into squats, sprints, or shooting drills, let's talk about technique. Using the proper technique is important in order to prevent injuries and minimize the strain to your joints and ligaments. Before you do anything, you need a stretching routine. Stretching before strength or basketball training will reduce your muscle soreness post-workout and optimize your workout results. Stretching will also help to keep you limber, which is a plus in basketball because it allows you to make more agile moves on the court.

There are two different types of stretches: dynamic and static. A dynamic stretch is stretching in motion. These types of stretches are beneficial to you as an athlete as they activate the muscles you will use during your workout, extend your range of motion, and enhance your muscular power. An example is jogging in place with high knees. This stretch emulates running down the court and shooting a one-footed layup. It will warm up the muscles in your legs and improve your range of motion.

Static stretches are the stretches that come to mind when you ask most people what a stretch is. They are the stretches that you hold for a certain amount of time in a fixed position. Static stretches are beneficial because they improve flexibility, alleviate muscle soreness, and are easy on your joints.

Keep in mind that stretching should be done both pre- and post-workout. You only need to spend about 5 to 10 minutes on post-workout stretching, but it is very important, so make the time! Post-workout stretching will help to release the lactic acid buildup in your muscles so you will be much less sore in the following days. It also relaxes you and reduces stress so you will be calm and focused for your next task of the day. An example of a post-workout stretch is the hamstring stretch. This is when you sit on the ground, extend one leg straight out in front of you, grab the toes of that foot with both hands, and hold for 15 to 20 seconds.

Sample Pre-Workout Stretching Routine

Shoulders, Upper Back, Chest

Stand with your feet hip-width apart. Put your arms down by your sides. Raise both arms and swing them to your front in a circular motion for 15 repetitions. Reverse and swing them backward for another 15 reps.

Raise your arms to the side with your upper arms parallel to the floor, forearms perpendicular to your upper arms and your palms facing forward. Pull both arms backward while squeezing your shoulder blades together. Next, bring both arms forward until your forearms touch in front of your chest. Do 20 repetitions.

Hips, Obliques, Lower Back

Place your hands on your hips and perform hip circles, or hip twists. Move your hips in a clock-wise direction 20 times, then counter-clock-wise for another 20 reps. Next perform side bends by alternately bending to your right, then your left. Keep your head up and body upright. Do 20 repetitions.

Quadriceps, Hamstrings, Butt, Calves

Stand with your feet slightly further than half hip-width apart. Place your hands on your hips and lower yourself into a squat. Ensure your feet remain flat on the floor and your knees are in line with your feet. Go as low as you can. Do 15 to 20 reps.

Sample Post-Workout Stretching Routine

- Quadriceps - Standing quadriceps stretch (15 seconds)
- Hamstrings - Standing hamstring stretch (10 seconds)
  - Seated forward hamstring stretch (15 seconds)
- Calves - Floor board straight leg calve stretch (10 seconds)
- Biceps - One-armed doorway biceps stretch (10 seconds)
- Chest - Two-armed doorway chest stretch (10 seconds)
- Triceps - Overhead triceps stretch (10 seconds)
- Shoulders - Side deltoid stretch cross chest (10 seconds)

Exercise Planning

Use this section to plan how often you will work out per week. Remember, you DO NOT have to go to a gym to work out!

Cardiovascular Exercises
Beginner - 2.5 hours per week recommended
Intermediate - 3 hours per week recommended
Advanced - 3.5 hours per week recommended

_____ hours per week
Circle: Sun Mon Tues Wed Thurs Fri Sat

Strength Training
Beginner - at least 2 times per week recommended
Intermediate - at least 2 times per week recommended
Advanced - at least 3 times per week recommended

Upper Body _____ times per week
Circle: Sun Mon Tues Wed Thurs Fri Sat

Lower Body _____ times per week
Circle: Sun Mon Tues Wed Thurs Fri Sat

Abdominals _____ times per week
Circle: Sun Mon Tues Wed Thurs Fri Sat

Basketball Training

Beginner – at least 2 times week recommended

Intermediate - at least 4 times per week recommended

Advanced - at least 6 times per week recommended

_____ times per week

Circle: Sun Mon Tues Wed Thurs Fri Sat

12 Week Roadmap Chart

	Week 1	Week 2	Week 3	Week 4	Week 5	Week 6
Date						
Shoulders						
Upper Arms R						
Upper Arms L						
Chest/Bust						
Stomach						
Thighs R						
Thighs L						
Hips						
Calves R						
Calves L						
BMI						
Body Fat %						
Resting Heart Rate						

	Week 7	Week 8	Week 9	Week 10	Week 11	Week 12
Date						
Shoulders						
Upper Arms R						
L						
Chest/Bust						
Stomach						
Thighs R						
L						
Hips						
Calves R						
L						
BMI						
Body Fat %						
Resting Heart Rate						

https://ATTACKBball.com/MAPWorksheets

Hurdles to Working Out & How to Jump Them

"Why do I have to put all this effort into working out? I just want to play basketball."

If you find the same routine boring, mix it up! Listen to music while you exercise, exercise with friends (this also helps you with accountability), or follow along with exercise classes or videos. Most importantly, HAVE FUN! You won't stick with a routine you don't like, so experiment with different options until you find something that fits your personality. The people who have fun playing basketball and get playing time are the same people who are doing the types of workouts outlined in this MAP. So, if you want to have fun and excel during games, I would suggest putting your efforts into finding joy in working out.

"I don't have time to work out."

Many people think that you have to drive to a gym and stay for at least an hour in order to get any benefits from exercising. This is INCORRECT! If you exercise for just 30 minutes a day you ward off colds, have more mental clarity, and improve your mood. When it comes to basketball, you can practice shooting for just 15 minutes per day. During that 15 minutes, you can easily take about 100 close range shots. Even if you only make 50 percent of them, you still watched yourself make 50 shots in a short amount of time. This will help you groove your shot (something I will talk about in more detail later in this book) and build your confidence. So, look at your daily schedule and see where you can **realistically** fit in 15 to 30 minutes of working out each day. By rearranging a couple things, I'm sure you can make it a priority.

"I'm too tired to work out."
This is an ironic excuse as exercise actually helps to increase your energy. Exercise produces hormones, which are short- and long-term energy suppliers. After exercising, you will feel relaxed and rejuvenated enough to enjoy family, friends, and hobbies. Regular exercise will result in a more energetic feeling toward life in general.

"I don't see results from my workouts."
Many times, we think that if we aren't losing weight or our basketball skills aren't progressing, we aren't getting results from our workouts. WRONG! This is where your planner comes in. By recording your stats on a weekly basis, you will be able to see your results in black and white. For example, you may see that the reason you didn't lose weight is because you converted your fat to muscle, which weighs more. If you have tracked your progress and still aren't seeing any results, it may be time to contact an ATTACK trainer. They are experts at developing new, custom workouts for you to ensure you are pushing yourself to the max.

"I have an injury/illness that limits my exercise."
Check with your doctor before starting any workout program. Most workouts can be modified and most medical conditions will improve with a consistent workout regimen.

According to the Centers of Disease Control & Prevention (CDC), exercise provides the following health benefits:
- Maintain or lose weight
- Lower risk of heart disease or stroke – two of the leading causes of death in the U.S.
- Lower blood pressure
- Improve cholesterol levels
- Reduced risk of Type II Diabetes
- Control blood sugar if you already have diabetes
- Reduced risk of colon and breast cancers
- Strengthen your bones
- Sleep better
- Increase mental clarity
- Reduce risk of depression
- Increase your chances of living longer

* All above information is based on exercising for 2 hours and 30 minutes per week

Monitoring Your Heart Rate

To gain full health and fitness benefits, you should work out at a reasonable intensity. Researchers have determined that the aerobic training zone is between 60-85% of your predicted maximum heart rate (PMHR). Note: If you are new to exercising, you want to calculate 50-65% of your PMHR. Your PMHR can be determined by subtracting your age from 220. To determine the aerobic range, multiply your PMHR by 0.6 and again by 0.85 (or 0.5 and 0.65 if you are a newbie). The chart below gives you an idea of the aerobic ranges for certain ages.

Age	PMHR	BPM 60% PMHR	BPM 85% PMHR	Target HR Zone 10 Sec Count
10	210	126	179	21-30
15	205	123	174	20-29
20	200	120	170	20-28
25	195	117	166	19-28
30	190	114	162	19-27
35	185	111	157	18-26
40	180	108	153	18-25
45	175	105	149	17-25
50	170	102	145	17-24
55	165	99	140	16-24

MY Target Heart Rate: _____ to _____

MY Target HR Zone 10 Second Count: _____

Why is the aerobic/target heart rate zone so important?

In order to get the most out of your exercise, meaning burning fat and seeing results, you should stay in your aerobic/target zone. If your heart rate is too low, you aren't burning enough calories. On the other hand, if your heart rate is too high, you will most likely not be able to maintain the intensity of your workout. This could lead to injury or giving up on your exercise plan, neither of which you want!

To take your pulse during exercise, stop what you are doing, and locate your heartbeat by placing your index and middle fingers on the inside of your wrist or to the left or right of your esophagus on your neck. Count the number of beats in 10 seconds to determine if you are exercising in your aerobic zone. If you are exercising too hard, slow down; if you are not exercising hard enough, speed up or add arm movements.

Finally, remember that your heart rate is just one tool to determine the intensity with which you should exercise. You *always* need to pay attention to how you feel and what your body is telling you. Find the sweet spot, that place which forces you do things differently than in the past but still encourages you to persevere.

How to Exercise If You Want to Lose Weight

So, which workout will help you shed pounds the quickest? The one that burns up the most calories, most efficiently. Cardio is king when it comes to calorie burning, and you'll see even better results if your workout has an "afterburn" effect.

Interval-style workouts (alternating between short bursts of high intensity effort followed by brief periods of recovery) are one of the best ways to turn on this afterburn, which means you'll keep burning calories hours after the workout is over. Any time you elevate your heart rate into the top end of your target zone, your calorie burn continues in order to bring your heart rate and muscle activity back to normal.

There are a few important things to note to maximize your exercise time for weight loss:

First, too much high intensity cardio can burn out your body, leaving you too tired to stick with your routine. To avoid this, alternate two or three days per week of higher intensity interval workouts with more endurance-focused sessions (exercising at an intensity where you can still talk without getting too winded).

Second, it's important to build lean muscle mass to help give your body shape and definition while you continue to slim down. For best weight loss results, do cardio 30 to 60 minutes, five days a week, along with two to three non-consecutive days of resistance training (this can be with weights, bands, or just your body weight).

Arguably, the best workout for anything (weight loss included) is going to be the one that you'll do! So, find a way to make fitness fun. Trade the treadmill for a high energy Zumba class or shift from weight machines to using resistance bands to prevent boredom.

And, if you really want to maximize your time, consider workouts that have both a strength and cardio element to them.

Information from health.com. Dr. Michele Olson, PhD, Professor of Exercise Science at Auburn University

How to Exercise If You Want to Increase Muscle Mass

The best exercises to build muscle fast are compound exercises. So, what are compound exercises?

Compound exercises are multi-joint movements that rely on the work of several muscle groups to move two or more joints. For example, the squat involves the work of both ankles, knees and hips and puts major stress on the quads, hamstrings, glutes, back, core, and calves. With just two to four compound exercises, you can get a full-body workout that will build muscle fast, while strengthening the whole body and improving your overall fitness level.

So, with that being said, the absolute best exercises to build muscle fast will always be compound movements like dead-lifts, bench-press and overhead shoulder presses that use free weights or bodyweight as resistance.

Another feature of the best exercises to build muscle is that they are usually those that allow you to use the most weight. The more weight you can handle for a particular body part, the greater the growth.

By moving your own body weight or your own body weight plus added resistance such as when you do a traditional barbell squat, you increase muscle fiber usage and nerve activity. This means the nerves are sending stronger signals to the muscles to recruit more muscle fibers. When you force the nerves to organize the action of a lot of muscle fibers at once, you allow for a lot of growth and strength to develop.

Also, you must bear in mind that your body will eventually grow accustomed to your routine, and you will no longer be able to increase weight or reps. This will usually happen within 8 to 12 weeks of using the same exercise movement. This means it is time to move on to a new exercise. The best thing you can do if you want to constantly build strength, power and muscle is to utilize four to eight of the most effective compound exercises per body part. Stick with those and rotate through them throughout the year.

You MUST train to muscle failure to build muscle fast! This happens in that last, almost-impossible, rep of a set. Stopping short of this point ensures that you don't "switch on" the growth mechanism for your muscles.

You MUST choose the right amount of weight! Stay within the rep range of 6 to 12 for your upper body and 12 to 20 for your lower body. If you can do more than this, the weight is too light; if you cannot do enough reps, the weight is too heavy.

Finally, do NOT strength-train for more than 30 to 40 minutes at a time. Training for longer than 45 minutes starts to increase the release of cortisol, which eats away muscle tissue and increases the storage of body fat. Limiting your strength workouts to this amount of time ensures that your mental focus will be high from the beginning to the end of the workout.

Information from www.2buildmusclefast.com

How to Exercise If You Just Want to "Tone Up"

When most people say that they want to "tone up," they usually mean they want to become leaner. Basically, they want to lose fat, and add a little muscle definition—but not so much muscle mass that they look like a bodybuilder.

In the fitness world, there is no real definition for "toning." Toning is simply a term used to describe the end goal, which usually results from a combination of basic weight-lifting and fat-burning.

I'm not sure who first pioneered the idea that heavy weights will bulk you up, but it's FALSE! Lighter weights will not help you "tone" better than heavy weights. In fact, because heavier weights build the strength of your muscles, thereby increasing your metabolism and burning fat, lifting heavier weights with fewer reps (8 to 12 on average) and working until you're fatigued is more effective at helping you reach your toning goals. Not to mention that it's more time efficient, too!

If you've been avoiding weights because you think that building muscle means that you'll bulk up, think again. When you lift weights that are challenging, you actually create micro-tears in the muscle fibers. These tears are then repaired by the body (this is where soreness comes from!), and in that process the muscle becomes stronger and a little bit bigger. However, because muscle tissue is denser than fat, adding a little bit more muscle to your body and decreasing your fat actually makes you look leaner—not bigger.

If you really want to lose weight and get lean, you should have a strength-training plan in place that works every major muscle in the body at least 8 to 12 times, using a weight that is heavy enough that the last two repetitions are darn hard to lift. Only then is the body challenged enough to change, grow and adapt, making you stronger and leaner. Lifting this way is also a great way to lose weight.

Information from sparkpeople.com

WORKOUT PLAN   DATE:

Strength Workout

Circle One:

Upper Body   Lower Body   Abs   Time Spent: _____

Exercise		Set 1	Set 2	Set 3	Set 4	Set 5	Set 6
	WT						
	REP						
	WT						
	REP						
	WT						
	REP						
	WT						
	REP						
	WT						
	REP						
	WT						
	REP						
	WT						
	REP						
	WT						
	REP						

Cardio Workout   Time Spent: _____

Exercise	Duration	Intensity Level (1 - 5)

https://ATTACKBball.com/MAPWorksheets

ATTACK

Basketball

Workout Guide

"Hard work beats talent when talent fails to work hard."
— Kevin Durant

How to Train for Basketball Independently

Most people only train on one facet of basketball on their own: shooting. Basketball is a sport where each individual player has to be effective on offense AND defense. You also have to be able to motivate and coach yourself when it comes to training. Therefore, you must "PLAN to work and work your PLAN!"

The duration of each workout is up to you and will be based on your goal. Do you want to get a little bit better or do you want to be exceptional? The time it takes you to finish your workout will vary depending on your goal for the day and your skillset. Over time, the confidence you are building in your skillset will allow you to finish your workouts in less time. You will notice that you have to repeat many of the same drills **multiple times** in order to develop muscle memory. This is perfectly normal!

Furthermore, when practicing new drills, you must adopt the slow-motion technique. This means you go through the movements of the drill **very** slowly and then gradually increase your pace to game speed. While doing this, you want to be aware of every position, movement, and feeling in your body. This will allow you to perfect your technique and master new concepts much faster.

Below is my recommended guide for you to follow to be effective on your own. The terms are listed below without explanations. If you are unsure of a drill, you can watch me perform all of the listed drills by going to the following link:

https://ATTACKBball.com/MAPVideos

<u>Warm-Up</u>

The warm-up phase should last up to 10 minutes. Pick seven to nine dynamic stretching exercises from the list below, or include warm-ups that you are familiar with or always wanted to try. As a reminder, the importance of dynamic stretches is written about in detail on page 37. If you are on a basketball court, you can choose to use half or full court for the warm-ups. If you are in your backyard, mark off a distance of 30 to 50 feet with cones, rocks, or whatever you can find. To give you an idea of the distance, it is 50 feet from the hoop to half court.

- ➢ High Knees
- ➢ Butt Kicks
- ➢ Jog Forward/Backwards
- ➢ Karaoke
- ➢ Knee Hugs
- ➢ Quad Stretch
- ➢ Squat Lean
- ➢ Frankenstein Walks
- ➢ Figure 4 Stretch (Hip-Flexor Stretch)
- ➢ Lower Body and Achilles Stretch

<u>Dribbling Drills</u>

Dribbling drills are so important because every offensive move you make in basketball requires dribbling. Everyone knows how to dribble, but very few players ever learn how to control their dribble. Like Kyrie Irving, who I think is the best ball handler in the world today.

Dribbling is a skill that requires feel, which is why I stress that you should reduce the amount of time you look at the basketball while dribbling. Players usually look down for two reasons:

1. They don't want the ball to hit their feet.
2. They lack confidence.

If you never learn to groove your dribbling, you will never gain confidence. Confidence is what allows you to dribble at a quicker, harder pace and allows you to become a well-rounded offensive player.

These stationary drills are designed to loosen your wrist muscles and allow you to familiarize yourself with how the ball should feel in your hand and on the pads of your fingers. You should pick a couple of stationary drills from the categories below before moving on to the on-the-move dribbling drills. Remember, this is just a guide. Be creative and use your imagination. There are very few distinct basketball drills, but millions of variations. So, if you do come up with a new drill, WRITE IT DOWN!

All dribbling drills should be done in the "hot stance":

- Shoulders over feet

- Knees over ankles

- Hips dropped/Butt back – You should be in a quarter-squat, which means you drop down about 12 inches.

- Flat back – If you are in the correct position, you should be able to place the basketball on the back of your neck and it will slowly roll down your back.

<u>Stationary 1-Ball – Right and Left Hand</u>
- ➢ Pound Dribble
- ➢ Front V/Side V/Sevens
- ➢ Crossover (Front/Back)
- ➢ Behind the Back
- ➢ Between the Legs
- ➢ Dribble Figure 8s
- ➢ Spider Dribble
- ➢ Drop and Catch
- ➢ Circle Circuit Series
- ➢ Wall Dribbles
- ➢ Wall Touch Series

<u>On-The-Move 1-Ball – Right and Left Hand</u>
- ➢ Continuous Crossover
- ➢ Continuous Ball Wraps Around Each Leg
- ➢ Pound Dribble
- ➢ Zig Zag Crossover
- ➢ Zig Zag Between the Legs

> ➢ Zig Zag Behind the Back
> ➢ Zig Zag Spin Move

Stationary 2-Ball

Two-Ball drills can be performed in unison or as offset (alternating dribbles)

> ➢ Two Ball High Dribble (Shoulder Height)
> ➢ Two Ball Mid Dribble (Waist Height)
> ➢ Two Ball Low Dribble (Shin High-Ankle preferred)
> ➢ Two Ball Dribble Low/High
> ➢ Triangle
> ➢ Triangle Pound
> ➢ One Touches

On-The-Move 2-Ball

> ➢ Pound Dribble
> ➢ Pound Alternating
> ➢ Zig Zag Crossover
> ➢ Zig Zag Between the Legs
> ➢ Zig Zag Behind the Back
> ➢ Zig Zag Spin Move

Shooting/Finishing Drills

This category includes layups, runners, floaters, and dunks. I define finishes as any shot within eight feet of the basket. Form is very important when finishing, which is why all of these drills should be done in the format that I teach: Slow down physically and speed up mentally. This means that in the beginning you should exaggerate your movement in slow motion so you can get used to the feel of the proper form. Once you have this down, you can speed up physically and slow down mentally, meaning you don't have to think about what you are doing, so you can give your all physically. Once you have mastered the form, you can easily pinpoint and tweak your shot if you begin missing finishes.

Finishes can be shot off of the square on the backboard, called banking. If you do bank your finishes, you should aim at the top corner of the square (top right if you are finishing right-handed and top left for left-handed).

No matter the angle at which you begin to make your move to the basket, ALWAYS remember to start square and finish square. This means your shoulders and feet should be pointing toward the baseline.

If you ever lose your balance going to the basket, are anticipating contact, or are avoiding help-side defense, the best type of finish is a two-foot finish. A two-foot finish:

1. Gets you back under balance and control
2. Gets you to finish strong by using your legs to power up
3. Gets you to finish high, allowing you to shoot a higher percentage shot

All of the finishing drills listed below can be enhanced by adding counter movements such as spin, behind the back, between the legs, etc.

➢ One Step Finishes (Use as a warm-up drill)

- o Layup
- o Runner
- o Floater
- ➤ X-Out Layups
  - o Jump Stop
  - o Reversal
  - o Shot Fake to Step Through
  - o Eurostep
  - o Floater
  - o Runner
- ➤ Chair Rips
  - o Left pivot blasters
  - o Right pivot blasters
- ➤ 7-Spot Layups
  - o Jump Stop
  - o Reversal
  - o Shot Fake to Step Through
  - o Floater/Runner

Post Moves

Stay low with a wide stance during all post moves. This gives you a base, which allows you to move more fluidly and makes it harder for a defender to get by you. The wide base gives you a larger range of motion and forces your defender to play you further away.

- ➤ Mikan Drill
  - o Reverse Mikan
  - o No Backboard Mikan (straight to the rim)

- ➢ Drop Steps (left and right foot pivots)
- ➢ Chair Pivots
- ➢ Up and Under
- ➢ Heel-Toe Turns (Right and left shoulder)
- ➢ Crab Dribble with Drop Step
  - ○ Up and Under
- ➢ Post Blasts
- ➢ Chair Post Circuit
- ➢ Jump Hooks
- ➢ Shimmy Turns (Shoulder Fakes) – Left and Right
- ➢ Combo Post Moves
  - ○ Mikan/Backboard Taps to Fake Post Blasts to Spin Move
  - ○ Backboard Taps to Post Blast

Extended Post Moves

- ➢ Two+ Dribble Drop Step Baseline
- ➢ Two+ Dribble Jump Shot
- ➢ Two+ Dribble Up and Under
- ➢ Two+ Dribble Running Hook Shot

Jump Shots

First you need to set the foundation for your jump shot. In order to do this, you need to "groove" your shot. Grooving allows you to form a consistent, rhythmic pattern. Do this by starting very close to the basket (no more than two to five feet) and making shots over and over again. This is also mental conditioning.

Another form of grooving shots is to utilize the side of the backboard. This not only helps you groove your shot, but also works on your accuracy. This doubles as a shooting coach as it allows you to see which way your shot is going. If your ball is bouncing off to the left, look at your feet and your follow through as they are most likely pointed that way and vice versa. The ultimate goal is to shoot off the side of the backboard and have the ball come directly back to you (a "clean" shot). Once you have completed 20 clean shots off the side of the backboard, you know you have correctly lined yourself up and you are ready to proceed with the shooting drills.

Warm-Up Shooting Drills
- ➢ Backboard Grooving
- ➢ 3 for 30 (Bank-Middle-Bank)
- ➢ 7 Spot Form Shooting (make 3 or more per spot)
- ➢ 3 Pointers (step into shot)

Combo Moves off the Dribble (Rip Series)
- ➢ Cross Over, Behind the Back
- ➢ Between the Legs, Behind the Back
- ➢ Spin, Shot
- ➢ Blast, Behind the Back, Step Back, Shot

Stutter Move Series (Drop Dribble)
- ➢ Cross Over, Behind the Back
- ➢ Between the Legs, Behind the Back
- ➢ Spin, Shot

➤ Blast, Behind the Back, Step Back, Shot

Roll Out Catch and Shoot Series
➤ Flair Screens
➤ Down (Pin Downs)
➤ Set Screen, Use Screen for Shot or Dribble Drive of Choice
➤ Floppy Screen, Use for Shot
➤ Back Up
➤ Circle Back/Fade
➤ Curl Shooting
  ○ In
  ○ Out
  ○ Shot Fakes, Dribble Drive, Shoot

Ball Screen Series
If you are the person coming off of the ball screen, you have to be very patient. I have included basic versions of ball screens, so think of other ways you can attack the basket utilizing a ball screen and incorporate those drills into your workout also.
➤ Split the Screen
➤ Shoot Over the Top
➤ Jump Stop, Fake Pass, Shoot
➤ Reject Screen (Go Away)
➤ Two Dribble Escape Pull-Ups
➤ Floaters/Runners
➤ Rescreens/Back Ups

Cuts to Get Open

Think escape on all of these moves and create space. You always want to attack the player's top/inside foot in order to get open.

- ➢ V Cut
- ➢ L Cut
- ➢ Go into Chest
- ➢ Inside Shoulder/Inside Hip Hold Off (drive down to pop out)

Conditioning Series

Each of these drills should be repeated about three times, with the third time being your best.

- ➢ X Drill
- ➢ T Drill
- ➢ Mountain Climber to Sprint
- ➢ Cone Pick-Ups
- ➢ 17s (sideline to sideline sprints)

Rebounding Drills

- ➢ Superman/Superwoman
  - o Put Backs
  - o Shot Fake Put Backs
  - o Up and Under

Basketball Dribbling Workout   Date:

Drill		1-Ball Stationary # Dribbles	1-Ball On-The-Move # Dribbles
	RT		
	LT		
	RT		
	LT		
	RT		
	LT		
	RT		
	LT		
	RT		
	LT		
	RT		
	LT		

Drill	2-Ball Stationary # Dribbles	2-Ball On-The-Move # Dribbles

Basketball Shooting Workout   Date:

Layup Drill	Right Hand Takes	Right Hand Makes	Left Hand Takes	Left Hand Makes

Extended Post Moves	Makes	Intensity

Jump Shots	Makes	Intensity

Combo Moves off the Dribble	Makes	Intensity

Catch & Shoot	Makes	Intensity

Ball Screen	Makes	Intensity

Bonus Basketball Workouts   **Date:**

Drill		
Cuts to Get Open	**Reps**	**Intensity**
Conditioning	**Reps**	**Intensity**
Rebounding	**Reps**	**Intensity**

https://ATTACKBball.com/MAPWorksheets

Your intensity level should be rated on a scale from 1 to 5 with 5 being the most intense and 1 being the least. And be honest! You are only holding yourself back.

What

About

Nutrition?

You Are What You Eat

Remember, you can't out-exercise your diet! If majority of your diet consists of eating pizza, cheeseburgers, and donuts, it should be no secret why you feel lethargic. Eating a balanced diet can protect you from health problems and help you live longer. Eating foods with certain vitamins also gives you more energy and makes your bones stronger. This is important in basketball when it comes to being faster than your opponent and avoiding injuries.

The good news is that if you aren't used to eating a healthy diet, you can make gradual changes in order to improve the way you eat in the long run.

Everyone goes to eat out at a restaurant. And with busy schedules, more than likely those restaurants will include fast food establishments. The great news is that you can still make good choices if you are grabbing something to eat on the run. I recommend the HealthyOut Healthy Meal Finder app, which can be downloaded for free on both Android and iPhone. This app lets you set up your profile and record your dietary preferences. Based on that, it will recommend healthy options from the menu where you are dining.

Finally, don't forget about the liquids you take in! Sodas, sports drinks, and juices contain LOTS of sugar, which your body converts into fat. And although it may give you an immediate energy burst, in a couple hours you will "crash" and your body will crave more. Better options are coconut water or organic fruit juice. However, nothing beats good old water!

Why Is It Important to Drink Water?

Did you know that water comprises 60 percent of your body weight if you are male and 55 percent if you are female? Water keeps every part of your body working properly. It helps your body flush waste and stay at the right temperature. You constantly lose water throughout the day through breathing, sweating, urination, etc., and you need to replace what you have lost. In addition to just drinking, you can also get water through eating certain fruits and veggies, for example, watermelon and lettuce.

The amount of water you should drink depends on your weight, the climate you live in, and how active you are. The easiest way to determine if you are drinking enough water is to look at the color of your urine. If it's pale yellow or clear, you are on the right track. If it's darker yellow, you need to step up your water intake.

A good formula to determine how much water you should drink is as follows:

Your Weight (lbs.) ÷ 2 = Oz of water per day

My weight _____ ÷ 2 = _____ oz of water

If applicable: Add an additional 8 oz of water for every 25 pounds you need to lose

Make sure you keep this number in mind each day. It is a good idea to carry around a water bottle with you at all times so you always have water with you. Also, this way you can break your intake number down into manageable amounts. For example, if you need to drink 96 oz of water per day and you have a 16 oz water bottle, then you need to drink six 16 oz bottles per day. You can divide this up by drinking one bottle in the morning, one at each meal, one during the day and one before bed. Easy and quenching!

How Do I Know How Much I'm Supposed to Eat?

I thought you might ask that! I am including the table below to give you an idea of the average recommended daily values for food for children aged four to adults. Keep in mind this is an AVERAGE. This means if you want to lose weight, you should eat fewer calories, etc. Or, if you are very active, you will want to increase the amount you eat so you are not starving your body.

Food Component	Daily Value
Calories	2,000
Total Fat	65g
Saturated Fat	20g
Cholesterol	300mg
Sodium	2,400mg
Potassium	3,500mg
Total Carbohydrate	300g
Dietary Fiber	25g
Protein	50g

What About Vitamins?

There are two groups of vitamins: water-soluble and fat-soluble. Water-soluble vitamins need constant replacement in our bodies, whereas fat-soluble vitamins (A, D, E, and K) do not. Fat-soluble vitamins are stored in the liver and fatty tissues. Most people do NOT need to take additional vitamin supplements IF they are eating a well-balanced diet. In fact, if your levels of vitamins A, D, E or K are too high, you can put yourself at risk for getting very sick. Below is a table of the recommended daily values for various vitamins.

Food Component	Daily Value
Vitamin A	5,000 IU
Vitamin C	60mg
Calcium	1,000mg
Iron	18mg
Vitamin D	400 IU
Vitamin E	30 IU
Vitamin K	80 micrograms
Thiamin	1.5mg
Riboflavin	1.7mg
Niacin	20mg
Vitamin B6	2mg
Folate	400 micrograms
Vitamin B12	6 micrograms
Magnesium	400mg
Zinc	15mg

What Counts as a Serving?

<u>Grains Group</u> - Bread, Cereal, Rice, and Pasta (whole grain and refined)
- ➢ 1 slice of bread
- ➢ 1 cup of cereal
- ➢ ½ cup of cooked cereal, rice, or pasta

<u>Vegetable Group</u>
- ➢ 1 cup of raw leafy vegetables
- ➢ ½ cup of other vegetables, cooked or raw
- ➢ ¾ cup of vegetable juice

<u>Fruit Group</u>
- ➢ 1 medium apple, banana, orange, pear
- ➢ ½ cup of chopped, cooked, or canned fruit
- ➢ ¾ cup of fruit juice

<u>Milk Group</u> – Milk, Yogurt, and Cheese
- ➢ 1 cup of milk or yogurt
- ➢ 1 ½ ounces of natural cheese

<u>Meat/Beans Group</u> – Meat, Poultry, Fish, Dry Beans, Eggs, Nuts
- ➢ 2-3 ounces of cooked, lean meat, poultry, or fish
- ➢ ½ cup of dry beans or tofu counts as 1 oz of lean meat
- ➢ 2 ½ oz soy burger or 1 egg counts as 1 oz of lean meat
- ➢ 2 tbsp. of peanut butter or 1/3 c nuts counts as 1 oz of meat

Information from health.gov

Nutrition Plan

Many studies have found that people who actually keep track of what they eat have better success at losing weight, managing their diet, controlling their portions, and sticking to healthy eating habits.

It's not all about counting calories either. Keeping a food journal forces you to think about what you ate, when you ate it, and how much you ate. It also allows you to go back and celebrate your victories. For example, shrinking your portion size or eating more vegetables on a daily basis.

Use the following chart to track the foods you eat on a daily basis. Write in the foods you eat and color in the corresponding circles for each serving from a food group to track whether you are meeting recommended servings. Don't forget to include beverages.

You should also keep track of the number of calories and grams of protein, fat, and carbs that you eat every meal. Since there are so many different foods with a variety of preparation options, I would recommend using My Fitness Pal for this task. You can visit www.myfitnesspal.com to create a profile or download the app on your Smartphone. Either way, this will give you access to an extensive online database where you can search for specific foods, even items from many different restaurants. Once you find the appropriate food, you will be able to view the full list of nutrition facts for the food. If you download the Smartphone app, it even allows you to scan a product's UPC barcode and then provides you the full list of nutrition facts.

Remember, the provided food diary and My Fitness Pal are just two examples of how to keep track of your food and beverage intake. If you have a different method that works better for you, then stick with that. The most important part is DOING IT CONSISTENTLY!

Date: _____

Grains Group	○ ○ ○ ○ ○ ○ ○ ○ ○
Vegetable Group	○ ○ ○ ○ ○
Fruit Group	○ ○ ○
Milk Group	○ ○
Meat/Beans Group	○ ○

Breakfast	
Snack	
Lunch	
Snack	
Dinner	
Snack	

https://ATTACKBball.com/MAPWorksheets

20 Super Foods to Promote Weight Loss

Avocado – Eat one quarter to a half of an avocado at a time to get your dose of healthy fat to help quiet hunger. It's also packed with fiber and protein.

Banana – Slightly green bananas will fill you up and boost your metabolism.

Black Beans – One cup of beans packs a satisfying 15g of protein without all the saturated fat found in red meat. Other beans also recommended are: kidney beans, garbanzo beans, and white beans.

Blueberries – Pack 4g of fiber into just 1 cup and only set you back 80 calories.

Broccoli – Only 30 calories per serving and also has cancer-preventing powers.

BROWN Rice – Contains lots of fiber and resistant starch, which helps to boost metabolism and burn fat. It is also heavy and filling, but low in calories.

Carrot Juice – You will find lots of Vitamin A here which helps boost your immune system and keep you healthy.

Cheese – Fresh goat cheese and feta contain a fatty acid that helps you burn more fat. Look for cheeses labeled "grass-fed," as those will have the highest content of this healthy fat.

Chicken – Make sure it's skinless! If so, a 3 oz chicken breast provides you with only 3g of fat and Vitamin B6, which is important for processing protein.

Eggs – These often get a bad rap. However, they are loaded with protein which helps you curb your appetite.

Grapefruit – Eating half a grapefruit before each meal may help you lose up to a pound a week. It also helps lower insulin levels and is 90 percent water so it helps you eat less.

Green Tea – Hydrates like water, helping to fill you up. Plus, it has antioxidants which increase your fat and calorie burn. This means losing weight around your midsection!

Kiwi – This little fruit provides 75mg of Vitamin C and less than 50 calories.

Lentils – Great source of protein and fiber. A half cup serving delivers 3.4g of resistant starch, a healthy carb that boosts metabolism and burns fat.

Oatmeal – Very rich in fiber, which helps you feel full.

Oranges – This ranks highest among fruits when it comes to making you feel full. They are also only 59 calories.

Papaya – Just half of this fruit provides almost as much potassium as a banana and over 100 percent of your daily recommended value of Vitamin C.

Pears – Just one pear packs 15 percent of your daily value of fiber. But make sure to eat the skin as that's where the fiber is hiding.

Salmon – Great source of lean protein.

Strawberries – Great source of Vitamin C and fiber. They are good out of the package or mixed in a shake.

Nutrition Tips for Adding Muscle

To add muscle to a skinny body, you need to make sure you are eating enough to gain weight AND muscle. If you find that you are staying skinny and not building muscle, increase your daily calories by 250 calories per day.

In order to build muscle fast, you must supply your body with the nutrients it needs to grow. The quality of your calories is important; you can't eat fast food and expect to build muscle. And no, you don't need crazy amounts of protein in your diet to build muscles as suggested in magazines. You DO need more than the average person though, so use the following calculation:

Lean Mass Weight x 0.8 = Daily Protein Req.

For example, if you weigh 200 pounds and have 10% body fat:
200lb -20lb of fat = 180 lean pounds x 0.8 = 144 grams of protein

My weight _____ X My body fat % _____ = _____
(Lean Mass Weight)
My Lean Mass Weight _____ X 0.8 = _____ (grams of
protein needed/day)

Highest Natural Sources of Protein:
1. Any lean cuts of meat
2. 100% whey protein shakes

3. White meat or Poultry
4. Any raw nuts, peas, beans (not refried), lentils or legumes
5. Most fish and any seafood

You also need to eat about 1.5 to 2 grams of carbs for every pound you weigh.

Best Carb Choices to Build Muscle:
1. Oatmeal (steel cut is best)
2. Brown rice or quinoa
3. All nuts
4. All beans
5. Sweet potatoes (eat the skin!)
6. Whole grain bread or pasta (organic is best)
7. Fresh or frozen fruit
8. Yogurt

Carbs: Good, Bad, or Ugly?

Carbohydrates, or carbs, sometimes get a bad rap due to all of the low-carb fad diets. The key is finding the right carbs, not completely avoiding them!

All carbs are made of three components: fiber, starch, and sugar. For classification, they are broken down into two categories: simple and complex. Sugar is a simple carb, and fiber and starch are complex carbs.

Simple carbs = simple nutrition. Most simple carbs do not naturally occur, but are added to the foods we eat. Some examples are sugar, corn syrup, and fructose. Common foods that are filled with simple carbs that you should avoid like the plague are soda, packaged cookies, fruit juice from concentrate, and most sugary breakfast cereals. And yes, I know it is difficult!

Complex carbs are more nutrient-rich than simple carbs because they are higher in fiber and digest more slowly. The main sources of dietary fiber include fruits, vegetables, nuts, beans, and whole grains. Starch is found in many of the same foods as fiber. The difference is that some foods are categorized as starchy because they are higher in starch content than fiber. Examples of high-starch foods are potatoes, whole wheat bread, and corn. Complex carbs are key to maintaining a healthy diet, so it is worth taking the time to read the labels on the foods you eat.

The fact is that carbs are one of the most important nutrients needed in an athlete's diet. They provide the main source of energy that our muscles, brain, and central nervous system use for fuel. Carbs improve athletic performance by delaying fatigue and maximizing muscle gain.

Athletes should eat carbs before, during, and after training. Before training, you should eat low-fat, high-carb foods in order to maintain your blood sugar and avoid an upset stomach. The best choices are yogurt or oatmeal.

During training, instead of turning to "specially formulated" sports drinks to keep you going, try organic apple juice. Apple juice will provide you with the carbs you need to continue training hard (56 grams in a 16 oz serving) but will save your body from all of the artificial ingredients in sports drinks. For training sessions longer than two hours, you can bring a snack, such as a KIND bar, for an extra boost.

After your training session, you need to help your body recover. You should eat your recovery foods within 30 minutes after the conclusion of your training to maximize the effects on your muscles. Now is the time to load up on high-fiber, or complex, carbs. Protein will also help repair your muscles, so ideal recovery foods will contain both high-fiber carbs and protein. Examples of great post-workout meals are a protein shake made with almond milk or a bowl of lentil soup with a piece of fruit.

Reminder: You should eat 2g of carbs for every pound you weigh

Your weight _____ x 2g = Number of carbs _____

Organic – What's All the Hype About?

Simply stated, organic produce and other ingredients are grown without the use of pesticides, synthetic fertilizers, sewage sludge, or genetically modified organisms (GMOs). Animals that produce meat, poultry, eggs, and dairy products do not take antibiotics or growth hormones.

Avoiding foods with added hormones is so important because hormones are the messengers for many of your body's functions, including growth and development, immune response, metabolism, and reproduction. Our body creates its own hormones to take care of these functions. But, eating foods with too many synthetic hormones, can interfere with your natural ones. This can then cause malfunctions within your body and lead to diseases such as cancer, obesity, diabetes, and asthma. So, when buying eggs, poultry, and dairy, look for products with the organic seal. When purchasing beef, look for packages labeled as grass-fed, antibiotic-free, or organic.

When it comes to pre-packaged or processed foods, my rule is that if you can't pronounce the ingredients, don't buy it. A processed food is any food that has been canned, dehydrated, or had chemicals added to it. Sadly, a whopping 60 percent of the average American diet is comprised of processed foods. Some processed foods are better than others. For example, a KIND bar is much better than an Oreo cookie. Below are the top 10 most toxic ingredients in processed foods that should be avoided at ALL COSTS.

1. Palm Oil – This is a type of trans-fat, which increases your "bad" cholesterol and risk of heart attack. Most fried foods are usually fried in this oil or something similar, so think twice before you place your order at any fast food establishment.

2. Shortening – Avoid this for the same reason as palm oil. You may also see this listed at partially dehydrogenated oil. Instead, choose foods that contain healthier oils like olive or peanut.

3. White Flour, Rice, Pasta, Bread – When a whole grain is processed, most of its nutrients are taken out in order for it to last longer. Because these grains are so stripped down, your body processes them too quickly and your blood sugar goes through the roof, which causes all kinds of problems in your body. Instead, choose brown or wild rice, organic breads, quinoa pastas, and oatmeal.

4. High Fructose Corn Syrup - This is a popular choice for manufacturers to use in place of sugar. It is in almost EVERYTHING! The problem is that it is even worse for your body than refined sugar, tricking your body into overeating and gaining weight. Read the label before you buy anything to make sure this isn't listed!

5. Artificial Sweeteners – These include things like Equal, Splenda, and Sweet N' Low. These supposedly diet-friendly sugar substitutes trick your brain into forgetting that sweetness means extra calories, making people more likely to eat sugary foods. Not to mention that they disrupt your normal metabolism and have been

documented to cause migraines, insomnia, and seizures. So, next time you have to sweeten your tea, go with either organic cane sugar or raw honey.

6. Sodium Benzoate and Potassium Benzoate – You can sometimes find these preservatives in soda, which you might want to think twice about drinking. These chemicals are known to cause cancer and are linked to causing serious thyroid damage. Stay far, far away!

7. Butylated Hydroxyanisole (BHA) – This can be found in HUNDREDS of processed foods to help the food last longer. It is also in food packaging and cosmetics. It is a potential cancer-causing agent and can seriously mess with your hormones. Follow my advice and avoid this like the plague.

8. Sodium Nitrates and Sodium Nitrites – These preservatives are usually found in processed meats like bacon, lunch meat, and hot dogs. They are believed to cause colon and prostate cancers and lead to diabetes. Make sure you check the labels to find meats that say, "Nitrate or nitrite free."

9. Blue, Green, Red, and Yellow – Artificial colors blue 1 and 2, green 3, red 3, and yellow 6 have been linked to thyroid, adrenal, bladder, kidney, and brain cancers. Watch out because these are in a TON of products. They can be found in medicines, fruit chews, pickles, juices, and the list goes on.

10. MSG – This is put in some foods as a flavor enhancer. Studies show that it can seriously mess with your brain

chemistry. So, play it safe and if you want to flavor your food, use salt (pink Himalayan is best), pepper, and other organic spices.

Data from www.thebetterhealthstore.com

8 Bonus Super Foods for Fitness

Beef – This food gets a bad rap, but truly lean beef is a great source of zinc, protein and iron. Your body absorbs the iron in meat much easier than the iron in other foods. Just make sure you pick the grass-fed leaner cuts: round, flank, and chuck. As a bonus tip, substitute your beef for either venison or bison for an even healthier meat.

Dried Fruit – This is a terrific source of energy and iron. They are fat free and have natural sugars so they make great dessert alternatives. Watch the labels though to ensure you avoid the ones that use artificial sweeteners.

Fig Bars – A favorite among athletes as they pack a strong carb punch and are easy to take with you and eat before exercise. They are low in fat and give you a little bit of fiber, too. Make sure to buy the ones without additives like high fructose corn syrup and red #5 dye.

Grapes – Good source of boron, which helps to build and maintain healthy bones.

Orange Juice – Besides being an excellent source of Vitamin C, one 6 oz glass provides nearly as much potassium as a banana and about 23 percent of your daily value of folic acid. Drinking a glass of this before a workout will give you energy through good carbs and natural sugars. Make sure to buy the fresh squeezed orange juice, not the kind from concentrate.

Pasta – Loaded with complex carbs for long-lasting energy. Wheat and quinoa pasta are always best, providing you with iron and important B Vitamins.

Potatoes – Probably one of the most misunderstood foods. Besides being a powerhouse of complex carbs, a 6 oz potato also provides twice as much potassium as a banana, one third of your recommended daily value of Vitamin C and 66 percent of your recommended daily value for iron!

Whole Grain Cereal – This is a great way to get fiber in your diet in the morning, which helps you curb your appetite throughout the day. It also provides lots of complex carbs to provide you with energy. Make sure you buy the organic type of this cereal as it will keep all of the unhealthy additives out of your body.

In conclusion, if you don't use this guide, you are NUTS! This guide is your roadmap, not only for basketball, but for everyday life. Think about it; I not only provided you with basketball workouts, I also gave you a step-by-step guide on how to best navigate to your goals. I provided tips to route you on how to train your body and mind, properly eat and drink, and how to set goals.

You WILL see drastic results if you follow this guide. Results will vary from person to person, but if you really apply yourself you WILL see a difference. I am not being cocky; it's the truth.

I know from personal experience that if you put the time in and get serious about your workouts, you can transform yourself into a great athlete.

So, what are you waiting for? There is no secret. Work works! Take your MAP and start your journey towards your final destination. I will see you on the other side of success!!!

"I've failed over and over again in my life and that is why I succeed." – Michael Jordan

"Work hard in silence. Let success make the noise." - Unknown

"When you're not working, just remember, someone else is getting better." – Coach Charlie Funk, Charlie Miller's High School coach

"Success is the sum of small efforts repeated day in and day out." – Robert Collier, Author

"Nobody's a natural. You work hard to get good and then work to get better." – Paul Coffey, NHL Hall of Fame player

"Commitment is a big part of what I am and what I believe. How committed are you to winning? How committed are you to being a good friend? To being trustworthy? To being successful? There's that moment every morning when you look in the mirror: Are you committed or not?" – LeBron James

"Most people have the will to win, few have the will to prepare to win." - Coach Bobby Knight, Charlie Miller's college coach

ATTACKBball.com

Made in the USA
San Bernardino, CA
23 May 2020